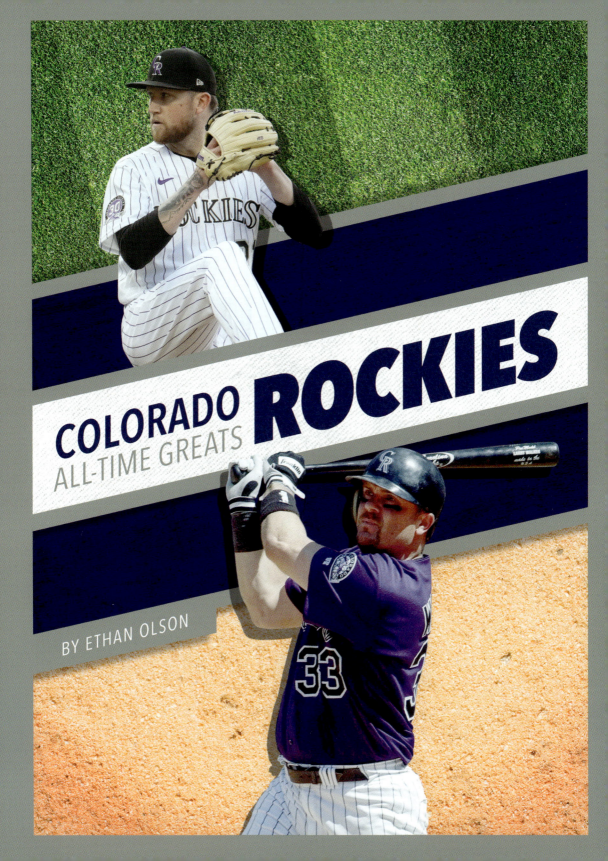

COLORADO ROCKIES
ALL-TIME GREATS

BY ETHAN OLSON

Copyright © 2024 by Press Room Editions. All rights reserved. No part of this book may be used or reproduced in any manner whatsoever, including internet usage, without written permission from the copyright owner, except in the case of brief quotations embodied in critical articles and reviews.

Book design by Jake Slavik
Cover design by Jake Slavik

Photographs ©: David Zalubowski/AP Images, cover (top), cover (bottom), 1 (top), 1 (bottom); Ronald C. Mondra/Getty Images Sport/Getty Images, 4; Brian Bahr/Getty Images Sport/Getty Images, 7, 15; Jonathan Daniel/Getty Images Sport/Getty Images, 9; Rob Leiter/Getty Images Sport/Getty Images, 10; Doug Pensinger/Getty Images Sport/Getty Images, 13, 16; Stacy Revere/Getty Images Sport/Getty Images, 19; Matthew Stockman/Getty Images Sport/Getty Images, 21

Press Box Books, an imprint of Press Room Editions.

ISBN
978-1-63494-795-4 (library bound)
978-1-63494-815-9 (paperback)
978-1-63494-853-1 (epub)
978-1-63494-835-7 (hosted ebook)

Library of Congress Control Number: 2023910235

Distributed by North Star Editions, Inc.
2297 Waters Drive
Mendota Heights, MN 55120
www.northstareditions.com

Printed in the United States of America
012024

ABOUT THE AUTHOR

Ethan Olson is a sportswriter and editor based in Minneapolis.

TABLE OF CONTENTS

CHAPTER 1
BLAKE STREET BOMBERS 5

CHAPTER 2
ROCKTOBER 11

CHAPTER 3
BACK TO THE PLAYOFFS 17

TIMELINE 22
TEAM FACTS 23
MORE INFORMATION 23
GLOSSARY 24
INDEX 24

CHAPTER 1
BLAKE STREET BOMBERS

The Colorado Rockies played their first Major League Baseball (MLB) season in 1993. The team had a talented core right away. First baseman **Andrés Galarraga** led the expansion team. In 1993, his .370 batting average led the National League (NL). It was the highest average by a right-handed hitter in MLB since 1939.

The Rockies traded for outfielder **Dante Bichette** before the start of their first season. On April 7, 1993, Bichette blasted the first home run in Rockies history. That was a glimpse of what was to come. Bichette's 40 home runs in 1995 led the NL.

Vinny Castilla was also with the Rockies from the start. The third baseman's powerful presence at the plate led to three Silver Slugger Awards in Colorado. That honor goes to the best hitter at each position in the league. His first came in 1995, which was also the first season **Larry Walker** played for Colorado. With Bichette, Castilla, Galarraga, and Walker providing

HOME SWEET HOME

The Rockies played their first two seasons at Mile High Stadium, home of the Denver Broncos football team. In 1995, the Rockies were finally able to play in their own ballpark. It opened on April 26, 1995. Dante Bichette made sure the wait was worth it. In the 14th inning of the season opener, Bichette crushed a walk-off home run. The fans in Colorado witnessed a perfect start in their team's new home.

the power, the Rockies became known as the "Blake Street Bombers." The name refers to a street near the team's ballpark.

Walker brought a perfect balance of offense and defense to Colorado. The right fielder's natural athleticism and instincts made him prolific at the plate. And his strong arm made him stand

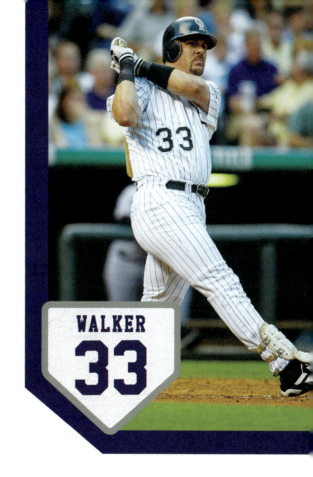

STAT SPOTLIGHT

CAREER BATTING AVERAGE
ROCKIES TEAM RECORD
Larry Walker: .334

out defensively. Walker's all-around play earned him the NL Most Valuable Player (MVP) Award in 1997.

Eric Young Sr. didn't bring the same power as his teammates. But the second baseman had immense speed that helped him steal bases. In his five seasons with Colorado, he stole a team-record 180 bases. That included a league-leading 53 swipes in 1996. Thanks to those impressive numbers, Young earned his only career All-Star Game appearance that year.

Ellis Burks rounded out the Colorado lineup. The outfielder had power like the Bombers, and speed like Young. In 1996, he became the first player in Rockies history to hit 30 home runs and steal 30 bases in the same season.

CHAPTER 2
ROCKTOBER

After some of the Bombers departed Colorado, the team reloaded with new talent. The reliable **Todd Helton** made his MLB debut in 1997. He would spend his entire 17-year career with Colorado. Playing as a first baseman, Helton used his athletic 6-foot-2 (188 cm) frame to win three Gold Glove Awards. That honor is given to the best defensive player

> **STAT SPOTLIGHT**
>
> **CAREER HITS**
> ROCKIES TEAM RECORD
> **Todd Helton: 2,519**

at each position. Helton was a complete hitter as well. When he retired in 2013, he led the team in hits, runs, and home runs.

Brian Fuentes struggled when the Rockies traded for him in 2001. But by 2005, he was the team's regular closer. His unusual sidearm pitching style confused hitters. It helped Fuentes become a three-time All-Star with Colorado.

The Rockies got a boost when **Matt Holliday** made his debut in 2004. Early in his career, the left fielder improved each season. It all came together for Holliday in 2007, as he led the NL in hits, runs batted in (RBIs), and batting average.

Lefty **Jeff Francis** made his debut the same year as Holliday. The pitcher used his 6-foot-5 (196 cm) frame to generate powerful

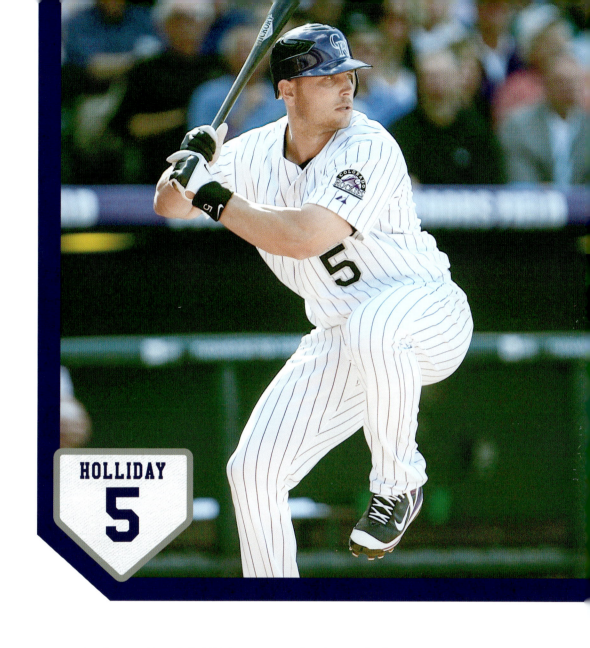

pitches. By 2007, he was Colorado's ace. He finished that season with a career-high 17 wins and 165 strikeouts.

Rookie **Troy Tulowitski** made an impact right away for the Rockies. The shortstop had a rare combination of elite defense and a powerful bat. "Tulo" helped the Rockies win 13 of their last 14 regular-season games in 2007 to set up a tiebreaker game for a playoff spot.

After beating the San Diego Padres in 13 innings, the Rockies swept their way through two playoff rounds to reach their first World Series. The team's dream run came to an end there, however. Colorado was swept by the Boston Red Sox. But fans still refer to that magical run as Rocktober.

UP THE RANKS

Clint Hurdle joined the Rockies in 1994 as a minor league hitting instructor before becoming the Rockies' hitting coach in 1997. When the Rockies fired Buddy Bell in 2002, Hurdle took over as the team's manager. After five losing seasons, Hurdle led the Rockies to their first World Series appearance.

CHAPTER 3
BACK TO THE PLAYOFFS

Ubaldo Jiménez was a rookie during the 2007 run. By 2010, he was one of the best pitchers in baseball. The righty's lightning-quick pitches were hard for hitters to deal with. He pitched the first no-hitter in team history on April 17, 2010.

That same year, outfielder **Carlos González** broke out as a star. "CarGo" could do everything at the plate. That was on full display on July 31, 2010, against the Chicago Cubs. González hit a walk-off home run to complete the cycle. He went on to win the NL batting title that year.

Starting in 2011, **Charlie Blackmon** began to play in the outfield alongside González. A reliable hitter for years in Colorado, the outfielder starred in 2017. He won the NL batting title and also led the league in hits, runs, triples, and total bases.

HUMIDOR HELP

Because of the high altitude in Colorado, baseballs tend to fly farther. This made the Rockies' ballpark one of the easiest to hit a home run in. Rockies management installed humidor machines in the park before the 2002 season. These machines kept the balls humid before gametime, making them easier to grip for pitchers. It also helped keep them from flying so far.

STAT SPOTLIGHT

CAREER TRIPLES
ROCKIES TEAM RECORD

Charlie Blackmon: 58 (through 2022)

DJ LeMahieu racked up hits for seven seasons with the Rockies. He had a big impact on defense, too. At 6-foot-4 (193 cm), he was tall for a second baseman. But his consistency in the field earned him three Gold Gloves with the Rockies.

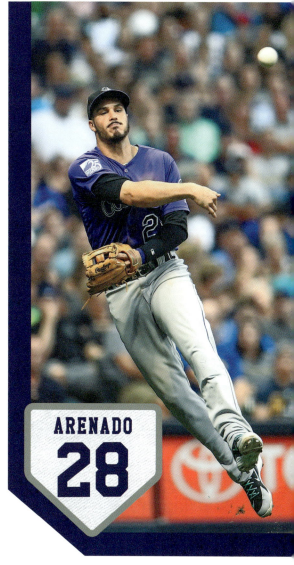

On the other side of the infield was **Nolan Arenado**. The third baseman's elite range and arm strength earned him a Gold Glove in each of the eight seasons he played with the

Rockies. While he was known for his defense, he could smash the ball as well. Arenado led the NL in home runs and RBIs in both 2015 and 2016.

Rounding out the infield during this era was **Trevor Story**. The shortstop's career got off to a historic start. In 2016, Story became the first rookie to hit home runs in his first four games. He continued a strong pace during his time in Colorado. In 2019, Story became the fastest shortstop to hit 100 home runs in MLB history.

Kyle Freeland grew up in Denver. As a kid, he watched pitchers give up a ton of home runs at Rockies games. By 2017, he was pitching for the team. Freeland was able to keep baseballs in the field of play. In 2018, his 2.85 earned run average (ERA) was the lowest in a season in team history. After missing the

playoffs for four seasons after 2018, players like Blackmon and Freeland gave fans hope the Rockies would be playing in October again.

TIMELINE

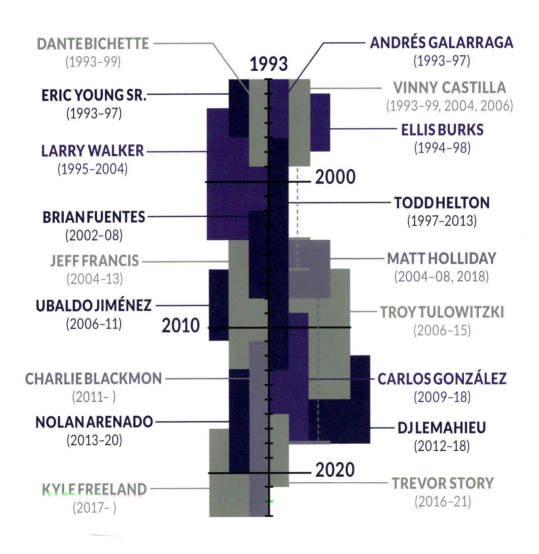

TEAM FACTS

COLORADO ROCKIES

Founded: 1993

World Series titles: 0*

Key managers:

   Don Baylor (1993-98)

      440-469 (.484)

   Clint Hurdle (2002-09)

      534-625 (.461)

MORE INFORMATION

To learn more about the Colorado Rockies, go to **pressboxbooks.com/AllAccess**.

These links are routinely monitored and updated to provide the most current information available.

*through 2022

GLOSSARY

ace
The best starting pitcher on a team.

batting title
When a hitter leads the AL or NL in batting average in a season.

cycle
When a player hits a single, a double, a triple, and a home run in the same game.

elite
The best of the best.

expansion team
A new team in a league, usually from a city that has not had a team in that league before.

no-hitter
A game in which a team's pitcher, or pitchers, doesn't allow any hits.

rookie
A first-year player.

walk-off
Any play that ends the game.

INDEX

Arenado, Nolan, 19-20

Bichette, Dante, 5-6
Blackmon, Charlie, 18, 21
Burks, Ellis, 8

Castilla, Vinny, 6

Francis, Jeff, 12-13
Freeland, Kyle, 20-21
Fuentes, Brian, 12

Galarraga, Andrés, 5-6
González, Carlos, 17-18

Helton, Todd, 11-12
Holliday, Matt, 12
Hurdle, Clint, 14

Jiménez, Ubaldo, 17

LeMahieu, DJ, 19

Story, Trevor, 20

Tulowitski, Troy, 14

Walker, Larry, 6-8

Young, Eric Sr., 8